I am Grateful

I am Grateful

A Workbook to Beat Anxiety and Stress

Jacqueline Bruce

SIRIUS

SIRIUS

This edition published in 2025 by Sirius Publishing, a division of
Arcturus Publishing Limited,
26/27 Bickels Yard, 151–153 Bermondsey Street,
London SE1 3HA

All illustrations courtesy of Shutterstock.

ISBN: 978-1-3988-5789-6
AD012273NT

Printed in China

He is a wise man who does not grieve for the things which he has not, but rejoices for those which he has.

Epictetus

Conjuring A Grateful Heart

Welcome to your very own book of gratitude, where you will learn how to reduce your stress levels by focusing on what you already have. Through making the most of your unique blessings, you will discover how you can nurture a more grateful heart. In a world of constant comparison with others, via social media and the internet, it can often feel as if you are lagging behind or that you are somehow lacking. Busy lives can mean more stress, while feeling overwhelmed is becoming normalized as a simple fact of day-to-day life, but it doesn't have to be that way.

In this journal you will learn how to take back control of your mental health and stress levels. You will explore what it is that triggers your stress response and how you can minimize those triggers. As a general rule, stress happens when you are overwhelmed, when you have too many responsibilities and too much to do in too little time. Feeling like you are running around in circles and getting nowhere is a classic indication that you are experiencing high stress. This in turn can lead to demotivation, lethargy, depression and anxiety, so it is important that you take the time you need to process your feelings. That is where the Power Insights in this journal can help.

Writing things down can help to free up space in your mind, allowing a sense of calm to settle in, where before there was only worry and anxiety. When your heart, head and hand work together to respond to these journal prompts, it triggers a response from your subconscious mind. You are in effect communicating with your higher self, thereby bringing your thoughts back from the brink of stress and focusing instead on the blessings that you currently have which you might not have recognized. Remember that what you focus on is what you get more of. This means that not only are you working on your overall stress, in showing gratitude for the things you have, you are pulling in more of the same from the universe.

Writing is a form of alchemy because it changes the way you think. Writing things down helps you to see any negative patterns of behaviour or where you might be sabotaging yourself. It can also help to highlight all the positive things in your life right now, which is essential in any kind of gratitude practice. Practicing gratitude forces you to focus on everything that is going well, on those happy synchronicities and moments of serendipity that might otherwise go unnoticed. It is also nice to keep a written record of everything that makes you joyful, or to honour those moments when life gives you a wonderful surprise.

Are you ready to become the kind of person who lives a calm, peaceful and low-stress life? If so, then it's time to pick up your magical pen and write your grateful heart into being. Good luck and may your heart beat with happiness, peace and joy!

Serene blessings,
Jacqueline Bruce

Nothing is more honourable than a grateful heart.

Seneca

The Insights

Power Insight One

Something Vexes Thee?

When you are feeling stressed it is a sign that something has vexed you. It could be a work-related issue, an argument with a partner, misbehaving children, getting stuck in heavy traffic etc. Whatever it is, it was the trigger that has led to you feeling stressed, anxious and overwhelmed, so you need to identify it. Think back through the events of recent days and see if you can locate the triggering event that has left you feeling out of sorts.

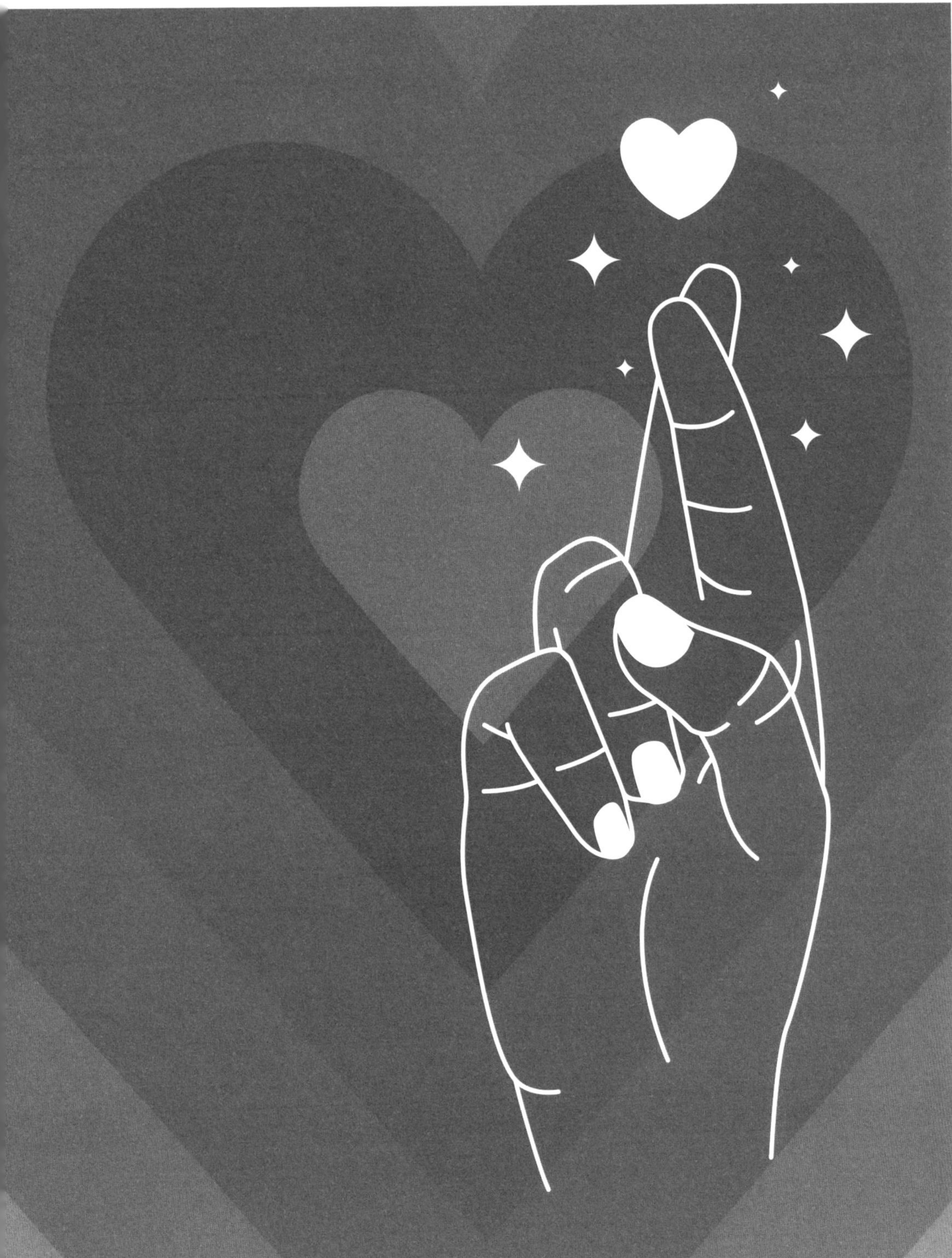

I started to feel cross when...

I felt challenged by...

I became overwhelmed when...

When... happened, I felt a shift in my mood that was...

Whenever I go to/see ... I notice that my mood drops or I feel ...

This is what I value most in my friends...

What do I find hard to forgive in others?

What do I find difficult to forgive in myself?

What causes me to feel instantly tense?

What are the methods I use to feel better when stressed? Do they work?

In what way?

Power Insight Two

Who Fights Your Corner?

The people in your life can have either a positive or a negative effect on your mood. Some will help to ease your stress, to calm you down and make you feel safe and capable of handling life's challenges. However, others will only add to your worries, be they a difficult boss or a nit-picking relative. It makes sense then to pre-determine who fits into which category ***before*** you interact with them. That way you can be ready for their influence on your mood. Make a list of all the people you see regularly, including co-workers, neighbours, friends and relatives, then answer the prompts below for each person.

Do I enjoy spending time with this person?

How do I feel after I have been in their company – happy, worried, anxious, inadequate, capable?

Can I describe how this person tries to lift me up or tear me down?

How does this person react to my stress and disappointments?

Are they around when I am succeeding and doing well?

In what way?

How do they respond to my triumphs?

How do they respond to my disappointments?

What is the main topic of conversation when I am with this person?

Would I say that they have a negative or positive influence in my life?

How could I spend more/less time with them?

Power Insight Three

Whose Stress Is It Anyway?

Make no mistake about it, stress is highly contagious! If you have been spending time with someone who has high levels of anxiety or unfounded fears, then it could be that you have actually absorbed some of ***their*** fears, leading you to feel unusually stressed. If this is the case, then it could be someone else's mood that you are experiencing in an empathic way.

Do you find yourself repeating someone else's words or phrases in relation to stress and anxiety?

Which ones?

Do you mirror their behaviours, such as hand-wringing, rocking or lip-biting?

Which ones? Does this only happen when you're with them, or have they become habits of your own?

Describe a time when you have picked up on the emotions of others.

I express my own stress in the following ways...

I express other people's stress by...

List out what you admire about the people whose stress you pick up on.

How does that person snap out of a stress response?

Can you lighten the mood when you're with someone who is stressed?

How does stress serve you?

How does being stressed serve others?

Can you think of ways to serve your emotional needs without stress?

Power Insight Four

You Are Blessed and Highly Favoured

Believing that you are blessed and favoured by a higher power can go a long way to making that your reality. This is because what you believe determines your behaviour and your behaviour determines your lifestyle. So when you think of yourself as being highly favoured and protected you will begin to act as if you are guided and blessings will naturally come your way.

I felt very blessed when...

What/who is the biggest blessing in my life right now?

A time in my life that felt miraculous was when...

A time when I felt divinely guided and/or protected happened when...

I find it easy/difficult to believe that good things will come to me because...

A miracle that came into my life was…

I have experienced the following miracles in my life...

The most recent blessing that came to me is...

which made me feel...

Which experiences feel enchanting to me?

Can you unlock any early memories that felt magical to you?

Have you been stargazing? Try it one night to see what feelings it evokes.

Power Insight Five

Daily Blessings

Good things come to you every single day, but you might not always recognize them. Some may seem so small and insignificant that you dismiss them as commonplace, yet they are still blessings and acknowledging them can help to lower your stress. Too often, people take the little things for granted until they aren't there anymore. Take some time now to consider all the small ways in which your life is a positive, pleasant place to be.

Something that made me smile this week is...

An unexpected kindness that I experienced recently was when...

I recently found...

Today a strange but wonderful thing happened...

Enchantment is all around me and I know this because...

Yesterday I was pleasantly surprised by...

Tomorrow I can spread happiness by...

I feel great joy whenever...

I feel abundant when...

I have food to eat, a roof over my head, warm clothing to wear, which makes me feel very...

What makes me feel grateful right at this moment?

I can share my blessings and gratitude by...

I am so happy that... is in my life

and that we...

Power Insight Six

The Bigger Picture

It can be all too easy to get so caught up in the stress of the daily grind that you forget to see the bigger picture. Your life is an amazing coalescence of intention, serendipity, choice and destiny. You are a miracle in your own right and your life is miraculous! The challenges you face have been sent to you because you have what it takes to meet them head on. Nothing is beyond you. You have great capability.

I felt very capable when I...

One of my main gifts/talents is...

I can use this gift to help others by...

My place in this world is important because I bring value by...

One person who benefits from my presence is...

and I make their day brighter by...

Where can I feel fear in my body and how can I release it?

One of my happiest memories is of...

I know that I am strong because...

When I was a child I wanted to...

and now I am able to do this by...

I can intentionally create...

I am grateful for the life I currently live because...

I can make improvements to my life by...

When I think of... I know that I have magic within me.

I know that each day provides its own gifts and today has brought me...

Lists of Note

Whose presence in my life causes me to feel joy?

Let us be grateful to the people who make us happy; they are the charming gardeners who make our souls blossom.

Marcel Proust

What do I love about where I live?

Acknowledging the good in your life is the foundation for all abundance.

Eckhart Tolle

Let gratitude be the pillow upon which you kneel to say your nightly prayer.

Maya Angelou

Which life experiences am I grateful for?

Who should I write a letter of gratitude to?

- ❍
- ❍
- ❍
- ❍
- ❍
- ❍
- ❍
- ❍
- ❍
- ❍
- ❍
- ❍

Gratitude is riches.
Complaint is poverty.

Doris Day

The power of finding beauty in the humblest things makes home happy and life lovely.

Louisa May Alcott

Which small, humble things make you feel happy?

What actions will I take each day to cultivate gratitude?

This is a wonderful day. I have never seen this one before.

Maya Angelou

When you arise in the morning think of what a privilege it is to be alive, to think, to enjoy, to love.

Marcus Aurelius